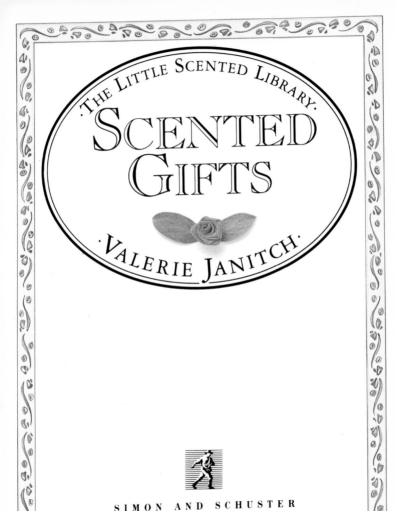

·THE LITTLE SCENTED LIBRARY·

SCENTED GIFTS

·VALERIE JANITCH·

SIMON AND SCHUSTER

NEW YORK·LONDON·TORONTO·SYDNEY·TOKYO·SINGAPORE

A DORLING KINDERSLEY BOOK

SIMON AND SCHUSTER
SIMON & SCHUSTER BUILDING, ROCKEFELLER CENTER
1230 AVENUE OF THE AMERICAS, NEW YORK, NY 10020

FIRST PUBLISHED IN GREAT BRITAIN IN 1991 BY DORLING KINDERSLEY PUBLISHERS LIMITED,
9 HENRIETTA STREET, LONDON WC2E 8PS

PRINTED IN HONG KONG

10 9 8 7 6 5 4 3 2 1

2

LIBRARY OF CONGRESS CATALOGING-IN-PUBLICATION DATA
THE LITTLE SCENTED LIBRARY.
P. CM.
INCLUDES INDEX
CONTENTS: LAVENDER / JOANNA SHEEN -- SCENTED GIFTS / VALERIE JANITCH --
POTPOURRI / MALCOLM HILLIER -- ROSES / MALCOLM HILLIER.
ISBN 0-671-73416-4. -- ISBN 0-671-73417-2. -- ISBN 0-671-73415-6. -- ISBN 0-671-73418-0
1. POTPOURRIS (SCENTED FLORAL MIXTURES) 2. AROMATIC PLANTS. 3. FLOWER
ARRANGEMENT. I SHEEN, JOANNA. II. JANITCH, VALERIE. III. HILLIER, MALCOLM.
TT899.4.L68 1991
745.92--DC20   80-19646

ISBN 0-671-73417-2

CONTENTS

3

INTRODUCTION

THERE IS AN EXTRA dimension to unwrapping a scented gift: an allure that is both instinctive and irresistible. Whether it is the heady fragrance of a garden in high summer, the earthy freshness of spring flowers after a shower of rain, the autumnal scent of woods and dry bracken, the intoxicating combination of citrus fruits, mellow apples and smouldering fir cones, or the wonderful aroma of fresh herbs and ground spices, scents can conjure up precious memories in a nostalgic evocation of times past. All these delicious, natural perfumes can be captured and used in many delightful ways in the making of fragrant gifts.

Summer flowers, perpetuated in pot-pourri, make lovely gifts. Present them either as they are or enclosed in pretty sachets, pincushions or pillows. Summer fruits, tastefully preserved, give equal enjoyment and satisfaction.

Whether you want to give pleasure to people by inspiring romance, evoking the past or whetting the appetite, this little book offers you a whole range of suggestions to help make your present-giving so much more worthwhile and especially thoughtful.

TRADITIONAL SCENTS

*I*N CENTURIES PAST, women combined herbs, flowers, and spices in ingenious ways to help mask many unpleasant odors. Posies of scented flowers were carried outside, while pomanders kept wardrobes smelling fresh and free of moths. Both posies and pomanders look attractive and are easy to make.

PUNGENT POMANDER

This wonderfully aromatic
pomander makes an excellent
moth deterrent. Simply stud an
orange with cloves, roll it in
ground orris root, let it dry for
several days in a paper bag, then
band it with velvet and lace.

NOSTALGIC NOSEGAY

Made from dried flowers, potpourri,
ribbon, and lace, this tussie mussie
(opposite) is reminiscent of
traditional nosegays that were
carried to ward off infection and
evil smells. Here, the sweet scent is
provided by the net bag of potpourri
in the center. Tussie mussies can be
made from fresh flowers and herbs.

FLORAL POMANDER

Dried flowers and ribbons decorate
this old-fashioned pomander.

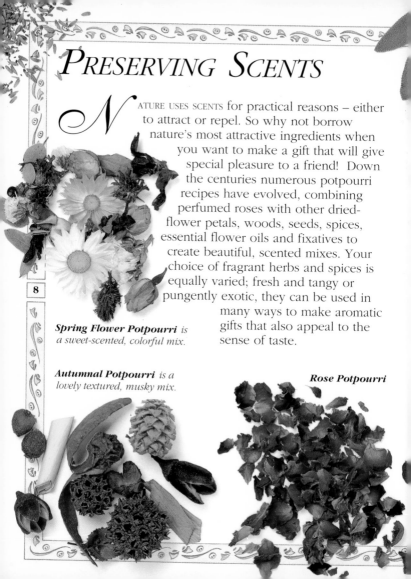

PRESERVING SCENTS

NATURE USES SCENTS for practical reasons – either to attract or repel. So why not borrow nature's most attractive ingredients when you want to make a gift that will give special pleasure to a friend! Down the centuries numerous potpourri recipes have evolved, combining perfumed roses with other dried-flower petals, woods, seeds, spices, essential flower oils and fixatives to create beautiful, scented mixes. Your choice of fragrant herbs and spices is equally varied; fresh and tangy or pungently exotic, they can be used in many ways to make aromatic gifts that also appeal to the sense of taste.

Spring Flower Potpourri is a sweet-scented, colorful mix.

Autumnal Potpourri is a lovely textured, musky mix.

Rose Potpourri

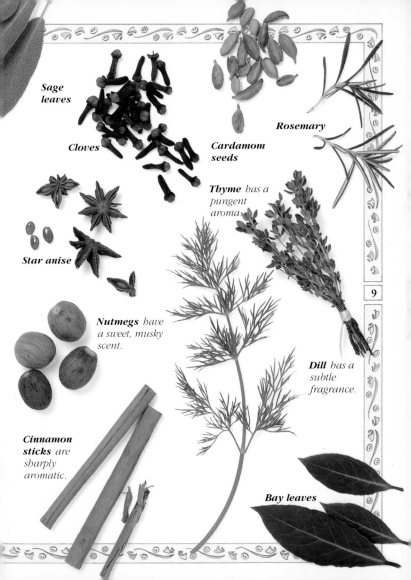

Sage leaves

Cloves

Cardamom seeds

Rosemary

Thyme has a pungent aroma.

Star anise

Nutmegs have a sweet, musky scent.

Dill has a subtle fragrance.

Cinnamon sticks are sharply aromatic.

Bay leaves

9

SUMMER POTPOURRIS

A FRAGRANT HOME IS A JOY to live in and a pleasure for anyone to visit. Use the abundant produce of your summer garden to create beautiful gifts of herbs and potpourri for your friends. Display colorful mixes of potpourri in unusual bowls, pots or dishes.

JUG OF HERBS
A bunch of freshly picked parsley, basil, sage, marjoram and coriander makes a simple and appealing aromatic gift (above).

SIMPLE ROSE MIX
Mix together 4 cups (1 liter) rose petals, 1 drop of patchouli oil, 5 drops of rose oil, and 2 tablespoons ground orris root for a mix with a rich, evocative perfume (right).

GARDEN FLOWER MIX

For a fresh, floral potpourri, mix together 4 cups (1 liter) mixed garden flowers and a handful of green leaves for contrasting color. Then add 2 tablespoons lavender, 1/4 cup (50 g) mixed sweet herbs, 2 tablespoons ground orris root, and 3 drops each of rose oil and carnation oil for a really fragrant mix. Place a bowl in the living room for a fresh, flowery scent.

YELLOW MIX

This fragrant, late summer mix contains 4 cups (1 liter) mixed tiny cones and yellow flower petals, 3 to 4 cinnamon sticks, and 3 drops each of lemon oil and pine oil.

SIMPLE POTPOURRIS

A GIFT OF POTPOURRI or dried lavender is even more attractive if it comes in an imaginative container. Craft and gift shops are often good hunting grounds for these. The rustic appeal of woven baskets or a miniature sack of grain emphasizes the natural charm of the contents, while the elegant shape of a seashell offers nooks and crevices in which to hide potpourri.

BASKET OF PETALS
Mix together two handfuls of fragrant dried petals from the garden, and add a few drops of rose and lavender oils.

SWEET LAVENDER
Dried lavender flowers make a simple potpourri all on their own. Place the lavender in a woven basket and decorate with a rose bloom. Add a few drops of lavender oil to strengthen the perfume.

HARVEST DISPLAY

Fill a tiny burlap sack with orange-colored petals, adding a few drops of bergamot oil for a long-lasting scent. Decorate the outside of the sack with strawflowers and grasses.

CIRCLE OF ROSES

Rosebuds and alchemilla flowers nestle amongst dark green leaves.

FRAGRANT SHELL

Although not strictly speaking potpourri, this tiny floral arrangement is scented with perfume which is hidden inside the shell. Soak a small piece of cotton batting in scented oil, then push it inside the shell. Fix some plastic clay in the florists' opening, then secure a few small dried flowers and foliage in the clay to decorate.

SCENTED SACHETS

AINTY, SCENTED SACHETS make delightful small gifts. Nostalgic and sweet-smelling, they are also useful for deterring moths. You can hang sachets in the wardrobe to freshen clothes, or slip them into drawers to perfume handkerchiefs and linen. Make them from fine net, voile, lace or cotton and fill them with potpourri or lavender for a heady fragrance. Trim your sachets with lace and dried flowers, gluing them in place with a clear-drying white glue.

MAKING A HANGING SACHET
Cut out a circle of cotton or net and gather up the edges. Fill the sachet with potpourri and tie with a ribbon. Trim with dried flowers.

HANGING SACHETS
These pretty sachets are filled with rose potpourri and trimmed with dried flowers and ribbons.

MAKING A FLAT SACHET

Cut out a paper pattern for the shape of sachet you would like. Pin this to double fabric, right sides together. Stitch around the edge of the pattern, leaving room for turning. Turn to the right side and, using a teaspoon, fill with lavender or potpourri, then close the seam. Trim with lace and ribbons.

FLAT SACHETS

Flat sachets are ideal for placing in drawers to add a delicate scent to your linen. These heart-shaped, circular and square sachets are filled with dried lavender and edged with fine lace, braided ribbon, satin roses, pearl beads and bows.

TEAZLE HEDGEHOGS

PRICKLY TEAZLES ARE POPULAR for use in dried-flower arrangements because of their interesting texture. You can also use them to make imaginative, sweet-smelling hedgehogs. The cloth body is partially stuffed with potpourri and, as well as looking decorative, it can serve a practical purpose as a fragrant pincushion.

MAKING A HEDGEHOG

1 Stitch a $3^{1}/_{4}$ x $8^{1}/_{4}$ in (8 x 22 cm) piece of fabric to a $2^{3}/_{4}$ in (7 cm) diameter circle. Join the back seam. Gather the top and 1 in (2.5 cm) below. Insert a cardboard base and fill with pot-pourri and stuffing.

2 For the apron, cut a $1^{3}/_{4}$ x 2 in (4.5 x 5 cm) piece of fabric and edge it with lace. Gather the top, then stitch it to the waist. For the shawl, cut a 4 in (10 cm) square of fabric. Fringe the edges and fold it diagonally. Remove any sepals left on the teazle.

3 Sew the teazle to the body of the hedgehog by holding it in place with long stitches over the top, caught at each side. Wrap the shawl around the scented body of the hedgehog and glue the corners over the apron to hold it in position. Cut a 4 in (10 cm) diameter circle of white cotton for the cap. Edge it with ruffled lace trimming and gather it $^3/_8$ in (1 cm) from the edge. Draw it up to fit the head of the hedgehog. Trim with a pretty bow. To complete the hedgehog, stick map pins or beads on the teazle for the eyes and nose.

17

ENCHANTING ORNAMENTS
In their quaint, old-fashioned costumes and pretty trimmings, these two tiny hedgehog ornaments would make ideal gifts for those who love nostalgia and romance.

SCENTED RAG DOLL

*S*TRICTLY FOR LITTLE GIRLS who have grown up, the perennial charm of the rag doll is epitomized in this very feminine moppet, demure in her candy-striped nightgown. What makes this rag doll special is her fragrant potpourri stuffing, which is hidden under her nightgown. Display your rag doll in the bedroom, where her rosy perfume can fill the air!

POTPOURRI BODY

To give the doll a lasting, fragrant perfume, make the area of its body below the shoulders from fine net and then stuff this firmly with a sweet potpourri mix. Try a mix of rose petals, lavender, ground orris root and bergamot oil.

DRESSING THE DOLL

Dress the doll in a romantic Victorian nightgown, gathering the wide skirt into a high yoke to leave the doll's perfumed body completely unrestricted beneath. Trim the underskirt with layers of delicate lace to give fullness, and then decorate her hair prettily with some roses, ribbons, and lace.

Display your rag doll in the bedroom, perhaps languishing on a satin coverlet on the bed or perched on a velvet bedside chair.

19

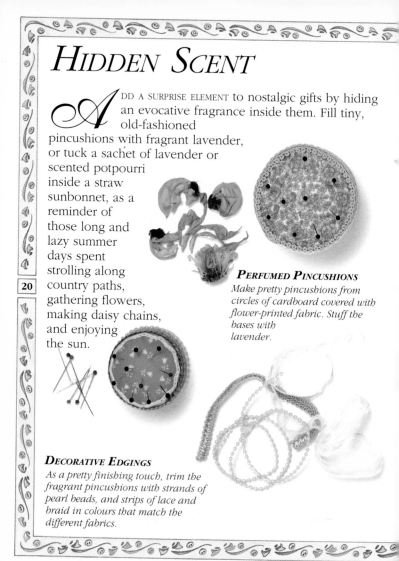

HIDDEN SCENT

*A*DD A SURPRISE ELEMENT to nostalgic gifts by hiding an evocative fragrance inside them. Fill tiny, old-fashioned pincushions with fragrant lavender, or tuck a sachet of lavender or scented potpourri inside a straw sunbonnet, as a reminder of those long and lazy summer days spent strolling along country paths, gathering flowers, making daisy chains, and enjoying the sun.

PERFUMED PINCUSHIONS
Make pretty pincushions from circles of cardboard covered with flower-printed fabric. Stuff the bases with lavender.

DECORATIVE EDGINGS
As a pretty finishing touch, trim the fragrant pincushions with strands of pearl beads, and strips of lace and braid in colours that match the different fabrics.

21

SCENTED STRAW BONNET

*A doll-sized straw bonnet
decorated with dried flowers
and ribbons makes an
unusual and romantic wall
hanging. Glue tiny satin
roses and sprigs of dried
foliage around the crown of
the bonnet, and then add
jaunty loops of ribbon and a
big bow. Suspend a gathered
circle of fine net, filled with
sweet-smelling potpourri,
inside the crown of the hat
for the fragrant surprise.*

FRAGRANT PAPERS

A SOPHISTICATED WRITING CASE, bound in richly colored pink silk and containing scented notepaper and envelopes, makes a thoughtful present – and gives any correspondence just a fragrant hint of romance! Cut out a folder of stiff cardboard and cover the outside with fabric, neatly overlapping the edges by about 1 in (2.5 cm). Cover a slightly smaller piece of thin cardboard in the same fabric, or use a contrasting color for variety if you prefer, to line the inside of the folder. Fix a pocket decorated with ribbon and lace to the bottom of the folder before you glue this into place. Finally, glue a pretty domed sachet containing a fragrant potpourri mix to the front of the folder. To perfume the notepaper and envelopes, simply store for a few days with a scented sachet.

SCENTED DECORATION

To make the potpourri dome, gather a lace-edged circle of fine net. Fill it with potpourri, then gather tightly. Press down firmly to flatten the dome, drawing out the lace to form a dainty rosette.

SLEEP PILLOWS

*L*ITTLE SATIN PILLOWS, lavishly trimmed with lace and roses and containing relaxing herbs, make charming gifts. Stuff the pillow with layers of fiber filling, then slip a muslin sachet of sweet sleep herbs between the layers. Lemon verbena, lavender, marjoram, rose, spearmint and cloves promote sweet dreams, while a spearmint, eucalyptus and menthol oil mix helps clear the

head and ease breathing. Other soothing herbs you can use include rosemary, hops, and thyme.

24

HERBAL PILLOW

This charming pillow is easily made. Tack layers of fiber filling to the wrong sides of two heart-shaped pieces of satin. Join the two pieces, leaving room to turn. Slip a herbal sachet inside before closing the seam. Top-stitch the edge, then trim with softly ruffled lace, strands of tiny pearls and satin roses.

SCENTED CUSHION

Made with pale, lemon-yellow satin and wide frills of old-fashioned cream lace, this pretty sleep cushion contains a soothing mix of fragrant herbs. The rosebuds are easily made from satin ribbon or may be purchased ready-made.

HERB GIFTS

*A*NYONE WHO LOVES TO COOK will welcome a gift of herbs: you can make dried herbs into attractive bags of *bouquet garni*, gather a bunch of fresh herbs, which will look pretty on the windowsill, or try making a herbal garland.

26

FRESH & DRIED HERBS

Fresh herbs look pretty displayed in a jug (left). To make the bouquet garni *bags (below), combine dried parsley, chervil, marjoram, thyme, and a bay leaf in circles of muslin and gather together with a bright green ribbon.*

HERB WREATH

Small bunches of fresh oregano, sage, mint, parsley and rosemary, intertwined with variegated grass and sweet-scented lavender, are wired to a wreath frame that has been covered with damp moss. The herbs will gradually dry on the wreath and can be used for several months. Simply snip off the required ingredients when you need them.

TINY GARLAND

Miniature sprigs of fresh parsley, sage, mint, lemon verbena, woodruff, hyssop, and lavender are first wired to a ring, and then decorated with the yellow flowers of the curry plant and green and white ribbons.

JAMS & PRESERVES

*H*OME-MADE GIFTS straight from the kitchen are received with delight at any time of year, while jams, jellies and summer fruits preserved in delicious syrup or liqueur have become a traditional Christmas present for the gourmet. Choose attractively shaped jars and top with a "mob cap" and ribbon for a farmhouse kitchen look. Try adding some dried flowers for an extra touch of the country.

28

GINGER ROOT IN SYRUP
Aromatic ginger root drenched in rich, sweet syrup makes a luxurious and traditional Christmas gift. You can make it look extra special by decorating it with fabric and trimming it with a ribbon.

RED CURRANT & GRAPE JAM
This jar of home-made jam is decorated with a cheerful spotted fabric, a red ribbon, and flowers.

PEACHES IN BRANDY

A jar of luscious peach halves immersed in sweet syrup and brandy makes the perfect gift for those who enjoy a little indulgence. Decorate the jar with a lace-edged mob cap and trim with yellow satin ribbon and dainty dried daisies.

HOME-MADE APRICOT JAM

A square of brightly checked cotton, fringed at the edges, makes a pretty cover for a jar of sweetly scented, home-made apricot jam, and a quicker alternative to edging fabric with lace. Ensure that the jar is airtight, then secure the cover in place over the jar with an elastic band. Finally, tie a colorful satin ribbon over the top of the cover for a decorative flourish.

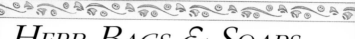

HERB BAGS & SOAPS

RELAXING BATH IS ONE OF LIFE'S greatest luxuries, which explains why gifts of soap, bath oil, skin lotion, and bath powder are so popular. Adding your own individual presentation gives the gift a specially personal touch. Search for attractive jars, bottles, and baskets in department stores, gift shops, florists, kitchenware shops, and even in flea markets. Fill the containers with pretty combinations of soap, herbs, bath oil beads, and home-made rose or lavender water, adding beautifully scented and colorful mixes of potpourri, lace trimmings, satin ribbons, and sprays of dried flowers to make them look unashamedly romantic.

HERBAL BATH BAGS
Fine muslin bags filled with dried herbs, trimmed with rosebuds and ribbons, and packed in a tinted glass jar, make an attractive gift. Loop a muslin bag over the hot tap of the bath so that the water runs through it, and relax in the herbal fragrance.

BASKET OF SOAPS

*A twig basket makes a
charming container for
guest-size soaps. Line the
basket with plastic and fill to
the brim with potpourri, then
trim with lace and let the
soaps nestle on top.*

SCENTED CANDLES

CENTED CANDLES CAN CREATE a romantic atmosphere in any situation. They are widely available, but it is easy to make your own. Add oil-based perfumes to the molten wax just before it is poured into the candle mold. Remove any ribbon decoration before lighting the candle.

YELLOW GLOW
The dye that you add to color the melted wax for your candle should echo your choice of perfume. A clear glowing yellow (left) suggests amber, lemon or pineapple scent.

ROSY PERFUME
Rosebuds and ribbons add to the attraction of this pretty pink candle (right), which is perfumed with roses.

HONEY SCENT

A sheet of honeycomb beeswax
and a wick are all that are needed
to make this intriguing candle.
Roll the sheet around the wick and
it is ready to light, smelling sweetly
of honey as it burns.

ORIENTAL CHARM

Spirals of colored ribbon pick up the
soft shades of this candle's floral
base. The oils used include
traditional lilac, lavender, jasmine,
violet, pine, cedar and gardenia, as
well as other oriental perfumes.

STRAWBERRY FLAVOR

Short and squat, this
strawberry-scented candle
stands on its own, with only
a pink-edged satin ribbon
bow for decoration.

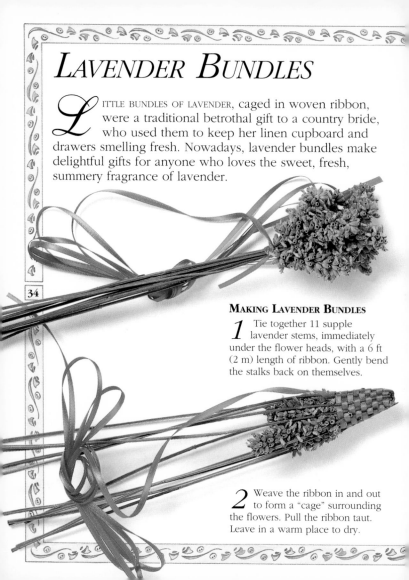

LAVENDER BUNDLES

*L*ITTLE BUNDLES OF LAVENDER, caged in woven ribbon, were a traditional betrothal gift to a country bride, who used them to keep her linen cupboard and drawers smelling fresh. Nowadays, lavender bundles make delightful gifts for anyone who loves the sweet, fresh, summery fragrance of lavender.

MAKING LAVENDER BUNDLES

1 Tie together 11 supple lavender stems, immediately under the flower heads, with a 6 ft (2 m) length of ribbon. Gently bend the stalks back on themselves.

2 Weave the ribbon in and out to form a "cage" surrounding the flowers. Pull the ribbon taut. Leave in a warm place to dry.

3 Draw up and tighten all the slack ribbon, then secure and trim it. Cut the stalks evenly to the required length. Bind the end of the "handle" tightly, adding a ribbon loop for hanging. Tie a bow at the base of the woven section using wider matching or contrasting ribbon. Finally, glue on a pretty spray of dried flowers.

STOCKING FILLERS

CHRISTMAS TREE AND FESTIVE TABLE decorations offer further opportunities for making tiny scented gifts. The jolly Santa, and his sack, are filled with orange and lemon potpourri – a real Christmas favorite. You can also make pretty little stockings, fill them with lavender or sweet herbs, and hang them on the tree.

SCENTED SANTA
Make the body from a cylinder of thin cardboard covered with red felt, and then paint and glue features on a ping pong ball for the head. To finish, give Santa a red felt hat and sack.

STOCKING TREATS

Make miniature Christmas stockings from printed cotton or chintz, and fill them with dried lavender, or aromatic potpourri, then neatly sew up the tops. Add a broad satin cuff to hide your stitches and attach a loop of very narrow ribbon to hang them. Then it is up to your imagination – and all those odd trimmings that you have got at your disposal – for the decorations. Ribbons, small pieces of lace, braids and tiny pearl beads have been used to adorn these attractive little stockings.

WRAPPING GIFTS

*P*RETTY PACKAGING IS A MUST for your scented gifts. The choice of wrapping paper is infinite, from all styles of floral papers to gift wrap made out of other materials, such as rice paper or metallic foils. The papers themselves may be scented in several ways. Try rolling up a sheet with a scented drawer liner, wrapping it in plastic, and leaving it to absorb the scent for a few days. Alternatively, wrap up the paper with a scented drawer sachet, or use a herbal tea bag for a lovely fragrance.

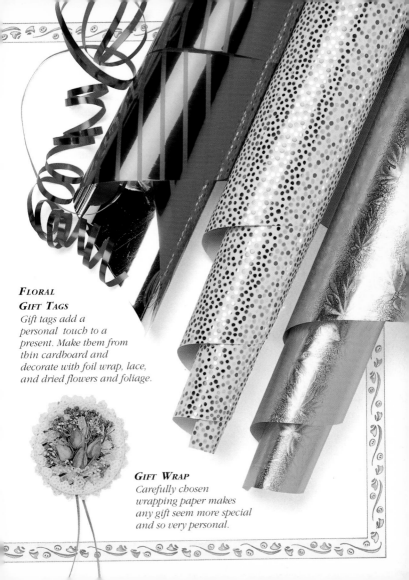

FLORAL GIFT TAGS

Gift tags add a personal touch to a present. Make them from thin cardboard and decorate with foil wrap, lace, and dried flowers and foliage.

GIFT WRAP

Carefully chosen wrapping paper makes any gift seem more special and so very personal.

INDEX

ACKNOWLEDGMENTS

The author *would like to thank the following for their help and co-operation:*
CANDLE MAKERS SUPPLIES, *28 Blythe Road, London W14 OHA, for the
scented candles.*
CULPEPER LTD, *21 Bruton Street, London W1, for their sweet sleep herb mixture.*
HALLMARK CARDS LTD, *for their paper-backed, colored foil gift wrap.*
OFFRAY RIBBONS LTD *for all the satin and velvet ribbons used in her designs.*
JOSIAH WEDGWOOD AND SONS LTD *for the loan of
Wedgwood china and Jasperware.*

Dorling Kindersley *would like to thank* STEVE DOBSON *for
his help with photography.*

Border illustrations *by Dorothy Tucker.*